YOUR KNOWLEDGE HAS VALUE

Bibliographic information published by the German National Library:

The German National Library lists this publication in the National Bibliography; detailed bibliographic data are available on the Internet at http://dnb.dnb.de .

Imprint:

Copyright © 2014 GRIN Verlag
Print and binding: Books on Demand GmbH, Norderstedt Germany
ISBN: 9783656728474

This book at GRIN:

https://www.grin.com/document/279060

Jari Niesner

The concept of daybreak in Larkin

A Brief Study

GRIN Verlag

GRIN - Your knowledge has value

Since its foundation in 1998, GRIN has specialized in publishing academic texts by students, college teachers and other academics as e-book and printed book. The website www.grin.com is an ideal platform for presenting term papers, final papers, scientific essays, dissertations and specialist books.

Visit us on the internet:

http://www.grin.com/

http://www.facebook.com/grincom

http://www.twitter.com/grin_com

Eberhard-Karls-Universität Tübingen

Seminar für Englische Philologie

PS II Cosmopoetics

WS 2013/2014

March 2014

The Concept of Daybreak in Larkin

A Brief Study

Jari Niesner

TABLE OF CONTENTS

Introduction

Philip Larkin, born in 1922, has been read under what are generally perceived as his major themes: death, fatalism and gloominess. However, throughout his life, he had constantly been struggling with and reflecting on problems of sex, marriage, love, and living (cf. Motion, esp. 291). Publishing four volumes of poetry by the time of his decease in 1985, Larkin became known for his lucid and often sharp-witted verse as well as for being socially withdrawn, sometimes called "the Hermit of Hull", where he resided from 1955 onward. His popularity among readers has not decreased ever since, partly because his observations stay true to a characteristic sense of experience in the modern world that most of his readers share. In the following essay, I will set out to explore the connection between shyness, indecisiveness, fear of death, and the aspiration to become an outstanding artist as linked to the concept of daybreak in Larkin, drawing mainly on his own writing. There will be two subsections: the first concentrating on his early writing, and the second mostly discussing one of his later and darker poems: "Aubade".

Early treatment of "dawn"

The North Ship, Philip Larkin's initial collection of poetry, is full of allusions to sunrise, morning, and daybreak, including a poem "Dawn" (one out of only seven in this collection with a title at all). Interestingly, a school magazine had already printed a short story called "Getting up in the Morning" five or six years earlier, when Larkin was at the end of Third Form (Motion, 22). Though literarily rather unimpressive, it provides evidence for his fascination with light and for his slowly but steadily developing melancholy. Whereas "Getting up in the Morning" contains a complaint about having to work when the day begins, "Dawn" handles its subject more symbolically. The speaker finds his heart "cold" and "loveless", like the outside world itself, which seems removed and "flying" away. Putting these pieces together, the sharp critic may already discern Larkin's growing elaboration on the curse of Adam – to use the cultural myth. In his eye, the world is a cold and barren place, which barely gives anything for free. The speaker in "Dawn" reacts with estrangement and passivity, a responsive figure iterated by many writers of the 20th century (among them T.S. Eliot, George Orwell and Samuel Beckett) to comment on the state of our common Christian Occident. Similarly, the seventh poem of *The North Ship* describes "morning" and "dawn" as decked with "the coldest dew", which a quick reader might mistake for the freshness of daybreak, and, accepting a wider conceit, as "frail and unsure". Perceiving the earth as "unearthly", the speaker is only sure in the fact that there's "no love". If these three pieces are considered a revelation of the poet himself, they clearly link to his shyness and inactivity. Larkin more than once claimed that "poems are about yourself" (RW, 49). In a world, where fluidity and indifference are the only realities, there seems to be no valuable action. At first, his dreams of being successful in either writing or life appear to be thwarted. Confronted with his shyness and slight stammer, they seem to be "hopeless / And keep[ing him] from sleeping". However, this poem germinates a different conclusion: "the sky spreads", "Earth [has] grown". Unreal, Yeatsian ("unearthly") and "silent" as it still is, his work begins to mature, or at least there is a flash of hope at the edge of its dawn.

The wish to go on is also a theme of "Nursery Tale", which features an intelligent pun. The first stanza comprises the story of a "horseman", only to take the poet to the ending in the knowledge that "failure [...] is the way of life" (Spurr, 63). Even "So[,] every journey [...] / Leads me [...] / To some new ambush, to some fresh mistake" (l.12-14); even though every journey is bound to fail, he nonetheless travels on (cf. Beckett's oeuvre). This perseverance is reinforced by the repetition of the word "carrion", becoming to mean "carry-on" as the poem closes, an insistent invisible voice urging not to give in despite the "weariness of daybreak" threatening his ambitions.

Two other works ("XVI" and "XVII") show morning and day as connected with the hope for change and the hope for emotional abundance. Both poems connect "wind" to volition, stressing the speaker's eagerness for motion and his latent energy. In the poem "XVI", the lyric persona is lying awake, expecting morning, after a long night of musing on sex, and probably betrayal (cf. the poem "Love Again"). He is at the same time waiting for the "voices of girls" and knowing that they are unattainable for him, dressed in "scarves around their heads". He seems to strongly resent that life is not going in the desired direction. Yet there is a sense of possibility, if also of dissatisfactory familiarity. A more positive emotional effect is created in "XVII", which foreshadows Larkin's career as a poet haunted by death. In his self-fulfilling prophecy, he "must visit the dead" in order "to write one song[,] sad as the sad wind". What he had not predicted, however, was the golden shine of the view of morning, its noise, its endless possibilities. He had not predicted 'life'.

The interlock of poetic ambition and life, and of the story of their opposition is perhaps most explicitly displayed in "XXII". Again, there is somebody waiting. Again, there is the activity of wind (as in the two poems before). The man "restlessly" moving about the "deserted platform" is Larkin, an unknown chap from the suburbs aspiring to be a poet. He seeks to explain to himself the origin of his ambition that will surely come to uneasy travelling through life, facing "a darkening autumn" already at its "dawn". However, the last line discloses that the embrace of lovers, or of a wife and child is the silence of a "sink[ing] grave". Looming behind his early verse was Larkin's idea that "what will survive of us is art", as W. Graham once summed it up altering a line from his "An Arundel Tomb" (Spurr, 71).

The following poem ("XXIII") makes clear his choice and repeats his gained knowledge that a "free [...] heart" "still end[s] in loss". He chooses art because it contains the possibility of survival throughout time. In contrast, he wonders in "Morning has spread again" whether love should not be given a second chance, having barely been tried an insufficient number of times. Here especially, the sight of "the red east expanding" arouses his "sense of life lived according to love" (CP, 86, Faith Healing). All these instances are proof of his vacillating attitude towards life and death. Later, in "XXX", he shifts in the other direction again using adjectives like "unripe", "bitter", "cold" and nouns like "uncertainty" and "shame". Writing seems but a "pastime in provincial winter". His shyness about his own talent and future leaves him without "confidence", the "unripe" day simply "plucked" and better spent indoors. The swift transmutation from summer to winter in this poem is an emblem of Larkin's changes of mood.

The first two cantos of "The North Ship" subtly and very tellingly address the "bargain" between life and poetry. *Legend*, to start with, recounts the tale of "three ships" heading for three different directions. Setting sails "in the morning", each ship is described as sailing to its own end, while two of them finally return home. One, however, is swept off to darker seas. It is the ship of poetry moving over the waters of Larkin's "proud unfruitful" unconsciousness, confronting "a long journey". Here again, 'journey' is a metaphor for life (like in "Nursery Tale"). Larkin seems to anticipate the gloom that later would deepen and increasingly shadow his life. The other canto, *Song 65° N,* is a fairly outspoken enunciation of the fear of death: The mariner centre-stage, who wakes with every daybreak afresh to the "waves fling[ing] loudly", dreads the impending voyage, "grow[s] afraid, / Now the bargain is made, / That dream draws close". What bargain is this? –The initial thought that comes to mind, of course, is the sailor's contract with the captain, or perhaps the charter of the ship. But as understood in terms of Larkin's own persona, this bargain is an offer of life for poetry. Poetry, like all other things, is "poise[d] on emptiness, on stars / Drifting under the world". It is a dream, yet maybe the only option to discard death and to gain eternity.

The bargain becomes even more apparent in "Waiting for breakfast", a poem written in 1947 and included in the 1966 reissue of *The North Ship* with Faber, when Larkin tackles the problem in the form of these questions:

> Are you jealous of her?
> Will you refuse to come till I have sent
> Her terribly away, importantly live
> Part invalid, part baby, and part saint?

The invocation directed at the poet's Muse is more or less an assertion of his decision. He asks whether the Muse, "towards [whose] grace [his] promises meet", will endure "a real girl" beside her (Motion, 127, 172). The word "invalid" and "baby" hint, however, at the instability of this decision. Larkin has not yet become the great poet he wants to be and is disenchanted with his poetry. "[O]nly when you choose" (i.e. the Muse) will he commit himself to literature (underscore added). The perpetual fight with these two opposing alternatives – "life" and "writing" – stems mainly from Philip Larkin's irresolution and timidity. Early on, it had been Sutton, a friend from school, who had urged him to take an interest in English literature (Motion, 22). The shyness of his parents, literary and "sexual frustration" are what I take to be the main reasons for the gloomier trait of his character (cf. Motion, 81). After all, Larkin was, like many of us, a person who had to love himself best and take his ambitions in his own hands, since he knew others, the time, were not to be relied on exclusively.

Not only in his poetry does Philip Larkin employ the image of daybreak, but also in his two novels, allusions to light and morning frequently appear. In spite of the differences between Larkin and the protagonist of his first novel *Jill*, it is possible to connect them by their social awkwardness. Although the author had acquired interpersonal knowledge during his years at Oxford, John Kemp remained a shy, clumsy personality and found himself confronted with an embarrassing situation at the end of the novel that was entirely his fault. Whenever Kemp sets out to seize the opportunity, he fails. Whether it is to become intimate friends with Warner or to approach a girl. This sense of failure is also Larkin's. Eventually, he must learn the lesson "that love died, whether fulfilled or unfulfilled" (*Jill*, 225).

Daybreak and early light play an important role in this novel as well. Crucial developments are often linked to dawn or are set in the morning. When Mr. Crouch discovers John Kemp to stand out in an essay on Macbeth, he reflects on a particular sentence of his future protégée like it was "a fancied streak of light in the sky before dawn: perhaps it was imagination, or the sun might be near" (*Jill*, 50). Again, it is Crouch here, and not Kemp himself, who "decides" he will excel in English literature. However, the ascension from the unknown towards excellence is "dawning". Larkin's literary ambitions seem to reach their fulfilment. Although it could only be an "imagination", there is the possibility of distinguishing himself. Further down the story, the protagonist finds himself unhappy in the morning after a night of drinking. Naively, he had believed "never [to] be depressed again" (*Jill*, 86). His tiredness and low state of mind still do not merely derive from a hangover but are a consequence of his spoilt ambition to gain status among his fellow-students. When his fantasies about Jill are not yet disappointed and the awareness of Warner's short-comings assuage his acerbic thoughts of being miserably unsuccessful, Kemp wakes in a more happy and tranquillised mood the next day (*Jill*, 164). This wavering between different moods as a sign of indecisiveness throughout the novel is splendidly described in the image of a swan he observes as he is roaming the town, unconsciously searching for Jill: "a swan, with a tempestuous beating of wings, half rose out of the water as if to break into flight, but then thought better of it and subsided back again" (*Jill*, 152). The swan becomes a metaphor of his desire.

At the end of the book, having pondered on the previous night with its drunken daring and fatal misbehaviour, and concluding death will come of every love, John Kemp falls asleep while his parents have just arrived to visit him in hospital. Despite his pessimistic view on the world, this final act of parental love leaves the reader to question his ideas. They need not be the ultimate truth.

In *A Girl in Winter,* Philip Larkin treats light, day, and morning in a similar way as he has done in *Jill*. Having been praised for its wonderfully composed structure, the former is divided into two major parts, the frame narrative and the story within. Whereas the action of the frame narrative happens in the course of less than a day, the flashback in the middle of the book comprises about three weeks. The novel begins with the poetic description of winter, as people get up for work, and ends when its protagonist, Katherine Lind, finds sleep beside Robin. This completely rounded-off story, which, in its sadness, is also very beautiful, is an affirmation of life. The short first chapter presents winter in a way that stresses its temporariness: people, though "unwilling", can cope with it. The concept of daybreak as an embarking on new endeavours intermittently recurs all through the novel. For instance, Katherine disembarks at Dover in the morning when she comes to England, a strange country for her, to stay with the Fennels (*A Girl in Winter*, 67). At another time, Katherine wakes early because of her restless mind brimming with thoughts of unfulfilled desire for Robin (*A Girl in Winter*, 128). While she walks around by the fields, she tries to warn herself about the ends this desire might lead her to.

In summary, Larkin's early concept of "dawn" is about breaking into activity. Although at times indecisive about life in contrast to writing, the wish to go on trying is ubiquitous throughout.

Late treatment of dawn

One of Larkin's last poems "Aubade", an uncollected piece first published in 1977, is among the most striking in the long tradition of aubades starting in the 17th century. Larkin's plain and unsentimental voice reveals the central theme of this poem already in the fifth line: "unresting death". It occupies him so much that he cannot distract his thoughts from it and guide them somewhere else until he reaches the final stanza. The inevitability of "extinction" scares him to the bone, and neither religion nor philosophy are able to provide any comfort. It "slows each impulse down to indecision". His shyness originates in his fear of death and the other way around. Had Larkin been a more out-going and positively extrovert person, he might have shaken off his gloominess. In fact, his parents had been rather "awkward people" (RW, 48), as he tells us in an interview with the Observer and is evident from his diaries (Motion, 26). Still, it would be wrong to attribute all of those dark states of mind to his genes. He deliberately chose them, leaning on the conviction that "being happy doesn't provoke a poem" (RW, 47). All his life he kept women at bay by entertaining always at least two relationships at a time, including his mother Eva (cf. Motion, e.g. 179), in order to feel free enough. Various expressions of his ambition prove the seriousness of his wish to be a writer (cf. Motion, 25, 106, 169). For all that, he stopped writing for a while after his father died (Motion, 173), let himself be distracted by work in the library (cf. Motion, e.g. 278), and cherished his relations to friends through writing hundreds of letters. Though opposed to the idea of marriage, he would finally live in a marriage-like partnership with Monica Jones (Motion, 498). After all, he could and did not hold 'life' at bay. He became an increasingly melancholy person, yes; he chose poetry despite claiming that it chose him, yes. But the depth and beauty of his poetry arise from the oscillation between life and death, from his indecisiveness.

Looking at "Aubade" again, its last stanza seems to say something very incredible in the grasp of this light: The "intricate rented world" brings complex emotion, work, ordinary life, and death. The day begins in whiteness, but also in the colour of the working people and, for all the grumble against life and the fear of death, cannot extinguish the work. The day might begin this way, yet we can still "be careful / Of each other, [...] be kind / While there is still time". His great, dark poem "Aubade" gives way to two last and more hopeful pieces: "The Mower" and "Party Politics" (cf. CP). The journey ends where it began. Every day, murky and obscure, will break with dawn. Perhaps nothing but blankness will remain of the man, but – as Philip Larkin was to prove – poetry will endure of the poet.

Works Cited

- Larkin, Philip. *A Girl in Winter (1947)*. London: Faber and Faber, 1975. Print.

- Larkin, Philip. *Collected Poems (ed. Anthony Thwaite, 1988)*. London: Faber and Faber, 2003. Print.

- Larkin, Philip. *Jill (1946)*. London: Faber and Faber, 1964. Print.

- Larkin, Philip. *Required Writing – Miscellaneous Pieces 1955-1982*. London: Faber and Faber, 1983. Print.

- Motion, Andrew. *A Writer's Life (1993)*. London: Faber and Faber, 1994. Print.

- Spurr, Barry. "Alienation and Affirmation in the Poetry of Philip Larkin". *Sydney Studies in English, Vol. 14*. Ed. G.A. Wilkes, A. P. Riemer. Sydney: University of Sydney, Craft Printing Industries, 1988-9. 52-71. http://ojs-prod.library.usyd.edu.au/index.php/SSE/index Web. 26 March 2014.

Declaration of originality

I hereby assert that the essay above is my own original work and that I have entered all outside sources in the Works Cited list.

YOUR KNOWLEDGE HAS VALUE

- We will publish your bachelor's and
  master's thesis, essays and papers

- Your own eBook and book -
  sold worldwide in all relevant shops

- Earn money with each sale

Upload your text at www.GRIN.com
and publish for free